CONTENTS

My Greek Traditional Cookbook 1

"Simple Greek Cuisine"

Original Favorites with Authentic Flavors

"Snacks, Dips, Meals, Sweets"

By Anna Othitis

My First Greek Traditional Cookbook

ISBN: 978-1496132192

Published by LionheART Publishing House

Dedicated to my amazing Greek mother, Chrisoula Galanakis and late mother in law Franga Othitis great cooks and teachers by whom I was taught to cook and bake.

And

To my husband and three children for whom I cooked and still cook for who have made this recipe book possible with their great encouragement and trust in me.

Living and growing up in Zimbabwe, Africa most of our lives we had the opportunity to always grow our own vegetables in our natural environment and surroundings. Everything we ate was authentic and naturally grown on our rich land. I highly recommend and suggest that the more natural and home grown the ingredients the more HEALTHY and NUTRITIONAL they will be for our HEART, BODY and MIND

Greeks love to celebrate life with an abundance of good healthy food, dance, music, wine and song. Modern research has proved that the traditional Greek cuisine is the heart-healthiest food in the world. Studies indicate the rural people of Greece and islands such as Crete and Karpathos have some of the world's lowest rates of diet-linked disease and obesity, and are among ethnic groups with the longest life expectancies. Growing up Greek in Zimbabwe, Africa with a big Greek family we enjoyed my grandmother's and mother's great healthy cooking and brought up my own family with daily Greek healthy eating. We always attended many birthdays, weddings, bridal showers, baptisms, name day celebrations (Saint's day), religious holidays, Christmas and Easter. There were our yearly Greek celebrations, parades, the annual "*glendia*" (festivals) of our fellow countrymen from around Greece, mostly Crete and the Karpathos Islands, where we inherited our family's Greek roots and traditions. With our "Big Fat Greek Family" of aunts, uncles, cousins, nieces, nephews, godparents and relatives through marriage, enjoying the Greek heart-healthy delicious home-cooked meals and celebrations seated around huge tables talking, laughing and celebrating with adults and children joining in: precious family times.

Greece has given the world much, from sports, architecture to philosophy. One of Greece's most valuable contributions is its authentic healthy cuisine.

At the core of the traditional Greek diet are the naturally homegrown dark-green leafy vegetables often gathered from the fields and mountains, including dandelions, spinach, mustard, fennel, cumin, fresh fruits such as figs, pears, plums, grapes, melons and oranges all handpicked from the homelands. Our foods are high in fiber such as whole grains, beans and lentils, carbohydrate-rich pastas and breads, natural rich extra virgin olive oil, olives, nuts, many herbs and spices such as garlic, oregano, bay leaves, cinnamon and cloves. There is scientific proof that delicious natural Greek Mountain Tea and herbs—chamomile, anise, mint, strawberries, honey and royal jelly are used for medicinal purposes and help in the prevention of cancer, especially breast cancer and osteoporosis.

Rich in immune-boosting antioxidants, the Greek diet provides cancer-fighting compounds, healthful omega-3 fatty acids and colon-cleansing fiber, which all help lower the risks of diet-linked diseases, including heart disease, obesity and diabetes.

A 2003 study conducted jointly by University researchers in Athens, Greece and Harvard University found that people who consumed a traditional Greek diet with products derived from the natural environment experienced a 33 percent lower risk of death from heart disease and a 24 percent lower risk of death from cancer.

Many Greek dishes are made with cheeses that are lower in fat and easier to digest than those made from cow's milk. Feta made from goat's or sheep's milk is more natural. The Greeks enjoy creamy goat-milk thick yogurt with fresh fruit with natural honey.

Greek cuisine is noted for its use of olive oil used abundantly in lamb dishes which are traditionally eaten on special occasions.

Greek meals include fresh sea fish - anchovies, cod, flounder and tuna in moderate portions. Proved in several studies, the omega-3 fatty acids in fish oils help prevent heart attacks and high blood pressure.

"The Mediterranean diet is characterized by a high consumption of fruit, vegetables, legumes, and non-refined cereals, a frequent consumption of fish, a moderate intake of alcohol, mainly wine during meals, a moderate consumption of milk and dairy products, mostly in the form of cheese and yogurt, and a low intake of meat and meat products. The Mediterranean diet is rich in monounsaturated fatty acids due to the liberal use of extra virgin olive oil. It is also characterized by high content of fiber, vitamins, minerals and natural antioxidants, while the content of polyunsaturated, saturated, and hydrogenated lipids is low." (Antioxidant Properties of Greek Foods and the Flavonoid Content of the Mediterranean Menu).

There are essential features of life in the Mediterranean that have spotlighted its cuisine as a tradition, that being the Greek appealing enjoyment of everyday life. Still kept and practiced, more so on the islands. The simplest of pleasures amongst the nation is the appreciation of healthy food relating to prolonged good health and life.

Greek mountain tea is also popular in the Mediterranean region and used as a tonic for a variety of health complaints, from colds to upset stomachs. The “Sideritis” family of tea plants from which the tea is made has been studied in the lab to investigate potential health benefits particularly due to antioxidant properties in the tea and the teas ability to treat ulcers. Studies have shown that a solution of 4 percent Greek mountain tea increased the total antioxidant power of the midbrain in mice.

Many refer to the Mediterranean Diet as the foods of the “Land and Sea” because of the ingredients that make up the method are derivatives of either or both. Foods that are from its natural source with it’s pure nutritional benefits.

"The Mediterranean diet is not only about what you eat. It's a way of life."

We hope you truly enjoy making and eating our delicious family recipes as much as we have enjoyed them and still do to this date. Using the most natural authentic organic ingredients without preservatives is the secret and key factor to healthy eating and success to our Greek cuisine

1. Avgolemono Soup

(Chicken Lemon Egg Soup)

This is a very popular traditional tasty and healthy Greek soup served and found on all menus in all Greek restaurants worldwide. This soup is made at most Greek holiday festivities.

INGREDIENTS

1 whole lean 3 lbs chicken washed and cleaned
12 cups water
2 carrots cut in half
2 celery stalks, cut in half
1 large onion, peeled and cut in half
2 bay leaves
1 tsp. salt
2 tsp. freshly ground pepper
1/2 cup orzo, pasta, or rice
3 eggs, at room temperature
1 tsp. fresh lemon zest
Juice of two lemons – strained

PREPARATION

- Take the first eight ingredients and add to a large pot. Bring the water to a boil then lower heat to medium low. Leave to simmer partially covered for approximately an hour.
- Carefully remove the chicken and vegetables into a bowl and strain the broth through a fine sieve into another clean pot. Return the strained broth to the stove and bring to a slow boil.
- Wash the orzo pasta place in the broth to cook uncovered on a slow heat for approximately 10 – 12 minutes until pasta has softened.
- In a bowl prepare the egg-lemon mixture. Use a whisk to beat the egg whites separately until very frothy, then add the egg yolk and continue to beat slowly. Slowly add the lemon juice and continue to slowly whisk.
- When the pasta is cooked, take the pot off the stove plate. Slowly ladle about two cups of broth and slowly add to the lemon-egg mixture keeping a slow whisk. Slowly add the rest of the hot broth to the egg-lemon mixture while continuing to whisk. This slowly minimizes the temperature of the lemon-egg mixture to prevent from curdling.
- Slowly add the egg-lemon mixture into the pot of prepared soup and keep stirring, mixing the egg-lemon and soup together. Return pot to a very low heat for approximately 5 minutes until soup is heated. (Do not boil the soup once the eggs have been added as this will cause curdling)

If desired, chop in a little of the carrot and a little fine chicken pieces into the soup.
Add more seasoning of salt and pepper as desired.

Note: If you like your soup thicker: Before adding the egg-lemon mixture you can add two tablespoons of cornstarch dissolved in a little warm water to the broth and stir in gently, leaving no lumps.

2. Faki

(Lentil Soup)

This is a healthy simple dish which is popular in the Greek villages, especially in the cold winter months. Served with feta cheese covered in olive oil sprinkled with oregano, olives and sliced baguette bread

INGREDIENTS

½ kg brown lentils
1 medium onion grated
3-4 sticks of chopped celery
2 large carrots sliced into small pieces
5 cloves of garlic roughly chopped
60 ml olive oil
2 bay leaves
Pinch of oregano
Salt and pepper to taste
White vinegar is optional

PREPARATION

- Rinse the lentils well in a colander under running water.
- Place the lentils in large pot, then add the onion, garlic, celery, carrots, oregano and bay leaves.
- Add enough water to cover the ingredients ensuring it is over and above by 2-3 inches giving the ingredients enough water during cooking time.
- Bring to a boil point then leave to simmer for at least 1 hour or until the lentils are very tender. If needed add a little more water during the cooking period, so there is enough soup content and not too dry.
- Add the oil, salt and pepper and gently stir.

Serve in soup dishes and if desired add a little vinegar to give it a slightly tangy taste. Served with fresh bread.

3. Fasolatha

(Navy Bean Soup)

This is a simple dish that is extremely popular. Another true healthy, popular and very traditional Greek dish. Simple to prepare and a tasty nutritious meal, served with fresh bread.

INGREDIENTS

½ kg haricot beans
1 large onion grated
2 carrots diced
1 tablespoons roughly chopped celery sticks
½ tablespoon tomato paste
150 ml crushed tomatoes with the juice
150 ml olive oil
Salt and pepper to taste

PREPARATION

- **Important**: Soak the beans overnight.
- The next day put the beans in a deep cooking pot with enough water to cover them.
- Bring to full boil and remove froth from the surface with a wooden spoon.
- Continue to simmer for 15 minutes.
- Remove the beans and drain them in a colander.
- Put the beans back in the pot and add enough hot water to cover the beans, adding more water to cover the beans above 2-3 inches.
- Add all the remaining ingredients and simmer for 1 hour or more – until the beans are cooked tender. Leave enough juice to form a soup.
- Serve in soup bowls and garnish with a little parsley.

4. Horiatiki Salad

(Traditional Greek Salad)

In summertime it is a popular Greek tradition to enjoy this (Horiatiki) salad, dunking your bread in the olive oil and juices whilst enjoying a cold light beer, glass of wine or a cold drink of your own fancy.

INGREDIENTS

3 medium tomatoes
1 cucumber
150 g feta cheese
5 Kalamata olives
1 small raw onion
Oregano
Olive oil

PREPARATION

The amount of ingredients depends on the number of persons to be served. The salad is very easy to prepare.

- Slice the tomatoes to a medium size
- Slice the cucumber in rounds or quarters
- Place all the salad into a salad bowl
- Slice the raw onion on top.
- Crumble the feta cheese on top
- Add the olives
- Lightly sprinkle fresh oregano on top add salt to taste
- Pour as much extra virgin olive oil as desired.
- Toss to serve

Note: If desired, add chopped pepper of your choice, small pieces of lettuce, baby spinach, *watercress* (is traditional)
Be creative.

5. Revithia Salad

(Garbanzo Bean Salad)

This salad is very cool and crunchy

INGREDIENTS

30 ounces Garbanzo beans washed and drained
2 cucumbers cut into quarters
12 cherry tomatoes halved
1/2 red onion finely chopped
2 cloves minced garlic
Crumbled feta cheese
Finely chopped parsley
15 ounces black olives drained and chopped
1 ounces Feta cheese crumbled
1/2 cup Olive oil
1/4 cup of Lemon juice
Salt and pepper to taste

PREPARATION

- Combine the beans together in a deep dish
- Add in the cucumbers, tomatoes, red onion, garlic, olives, cheese, parsley olive oil, lemon juice, salt and pepper.
- Note: Be careful not to add too much salt as the Feta cheese is salty.
- Toss together and refrigerate 1/2 hour before serving.
- Serve chilled in a salad bowl. Served with fresh crisp baguette bread.

This salad can also be made with a variety of beans mixed together to make a 3 bean salad.

6. Eliopsomo

(Black Olive Bread)

This is tasty nutritious bread that is simple to make. The olives give the bread that extra special taste. Try it with Greek salad or any of our Greek meals.

INGREDIENTS

150 g stone-less olives or un-pitted Kalamata olives
150 g wheat flour
150 g wholemeal flour
200 g strong white flour
9 g dried yeast
Grated onion (optional)
½ tsp salt
½ tsp sugar
½ cup olive oil
Lukewarm water to mix

PREPARATION

- Combine all the ingredients except for the olives; add enough lukewarm water to make a firm but pliable dough.
- Knead well for at least 10 minutes.
- Wrap the dough in cling wrap, place in a bowl and let it rest in a warm, but not hot, place to rise.
- When the dough is twice its size, place the olives in it and knead again for a few minutes to mix in the olives.
- Grease a 25 cm baking tin, place a little flour in the baking tin and swirl around ensuring the bottom and the sides are covered. Place dough in the baking tin and allow this to rise once more to double its size.
- Baste the top with a little oil.
- Bake in a pre-heated oven bake at 180 C degrees for 30 minutes or until golden brown.
- Let the bread cool in the baking tin then tip it over and place on a rack.
- Keep the bread in aluminum foil to keep fresh and avoid hardening.

7. Tzatziki

(Garlic Yoghurt Dip)

This is a classic Greek side dish, which can be served with meat or vegetable dishes.
Frequently used with souvlaki or gyros.

INGREDIENTS

1 cucumber
2-3 cloves of garlic
1 teaspoon medium wine vinegar
300g full-fat strained Greek yoghurt
100 ml extra virgin olive oil
½ tablespoon finally chopped dill leaves
Salt and pepper to taste

PREPARATION

- Remove the skin of the cucumber and coarse grate it.
- Grate the garlic into fine pieces.
- Salt the cucumber and leave it in a colander for half an hour to drain the excess water well.
- Place grated cucumber in a bowl; add the garlic and the remainder of the ingredients.
- Use a fork to mix all the ingredients well.
- The "Tsadziki" is now ready to pour into a bowl – sprinkle the top with a few finely chopped dill leaves.

Cover and keep refrigerated until served. This lasts in the fridge for quite a while.

8. Skorthalia

(Garlic Dip)

Greek Garlic Sauce - known as Skordalia - is delicious served with a variety of dishes, with beetroot, green beans, fried fish and more. Add olive oil to the vegetables before pouring the sauce on top. Use less garlic if desired.

INGREDIENTS

6 cloves of garlic
6 medium size potatoes
3 tablespoons lemon juice
120 ml extra virgin olive oil
50 ml of cold water

PREPARATION

- Cube the potatoes boil in salted water until cooked well.
- Remove skin from the garlic cloves and wash well.
- Place the cold potatoes and garlic cloves in a food processor, slowly add the oil and cold water and blend well.

If the sauce is too thick, add more cold water to soften into a paste, almost like a mashed potato consistency.

Serve the sauce on top of the vegetables, like beetroot, fried eggplant or zucchini, use as a side dish dip garnished with chopped parsley or a few olives. This dip is accompanied and very delicious with fried fish or a meat meal. This is also a tasty dip with pita bread and olives.

9. Keftethakia

(Small Meatballs)

The classic Greek meatballs are called *Keftedes* or *Keftedakia.* They can be eaten as a snack or can be a part of a buffet meal. They can also be a full meal with fries and Greek salad. Simple and quick to prepare.

INGREDIENTS

1 kg ground beef
1 large onion very finely chopped
Bunch of chopped parsley
A few leaves of chopped mint
2 slices dry, white bread soaked in water – well drained
1 tablespoon olive oil
1 whole egg
Salt & pepper to taste
1 cup plain flour
1 ½ cup vegetable oil for frying

PREPARATION

- Apart from the flour and the vegetable oil, mix all the other ingredients together well.
- Roll the mixture into small balls approx. the size of large walnuts
- Roll the balls in flour and then deep fry them for 15 minutes till golden brown on a medium heat.

Place on a paper towel to soak up the excess oil and then place in the dish. Serve garnished with finely chopped parsley.

10. Spanakopita

(Spinach Pie)

A very traditional popular Greek authentic dish which is a delicious healthy snack,

INGREDIENTS

For the filling:

1 kg spinach
250g feta cheese
6 spring onions
1 bunch fennel – finely chopped
2 tablespoons fresh mint – chopped
2 tablespoons olive oil
Pepper and pinch of salt

To baste the dough:

Egg well beaten with olive oil

For the dough:

300 g all-purpose flour
40 ml olive oil
2 finely chopped leeks
Pinch of salt
Lukewarm water to make a pliable dough
Ready-made Filo Pastry can be used in place of the dough

PREPARATION OF THE DOUGH

- Place all the dough ingredients in a bowl and knead well for 10 minutes. Divide the dough into three equal portions. Cover them with cling film and let them rest on a lightly floured surface for 1/4 hour.

In the meantime, prepare the filling.

SPINACH FILLING

- Finely chop the spring onion, leeks and spinach and put them in a pot with a little water. Bring to a slow boil to simmer until the contents are blanched until the water has evaporated.
- Remove from the heat and place in a colander to drain the excess water.
- Press the mixture with a spoon; this helps remove as much liquid as possible. Once drained place mixture in a deep bowl.
- Add the mint, fennel, pepper, crumbled feta cheese and olive oil. Add salt if needed – feta is salty anyway. Stir well and set this aside.

DOUGH

Prepare and brush the oven dish with olive oil.

- Using a wooden rolling pin, open the 1st filo ball into a flat round circle just enough to cover your baking pan/dish up to the top edge of the pan. Palace in the pan
- Lightly brush the first 'filo' with olive oil and sprinkle with flour. Roll out the second ball and place this on top of the first layer, making sure you bring the second filo to the top of the baking pan/dish edges, forming a pastry casing.
- Place the filling in the crust and even it out flat.
- Take another ball of dough and, with a little flour and the use of the rolling pin, open it out into a circle which is the same size as the top of the oven dish, enough to cover the top of the pan/dish.
- Place it on top of the filling to cover the spinach mixture.
- Seal the end by pressing the edges down with a fork dipped in water, using the fork prick the top of the pastry in a few places. (This is done so that the pastry does not rise and pop) Brush the top of the pie with olive oil and egg mixed together.
- Bake in a preheated oven at 180 degrees Celsius, for about 3/4 hour, until it has a nice golden brown color. Let it cool, cut into squares and serve warm.

11. Dolmades

(Stuffed Vine Leaves)

Dolmades can be eaten as a side dish. It can also be accompanied by plain Greek strained yoghurt or as a tasty little snack on its own. Ideally, the vine leaves you use should be the first tender leaves of spring or use the preserved readymade grape leaves sold in a jar.

INGREDIENTS

50 vine leaves – approx. 10cm diameter
(best vine leaves to use are the tender ones)
2 large onions grated
½ kg risotto/soft rice
1 bunch chopped fennel
5 fresh mint leaves chopped
Juice from 2 medium lemons
2 cups extra virgin olive oil
Salt and pepper to taste

PREPARATION

- Wash the leaves in cold water if using the bottled vine leaves wash to get the brine off.
- Place them in a large pan of boiling water for no longer than a minute – enough to soften them
- Remove the protruding edge of the central stem from each leaf.
- Place the leaves individually flat in a shallow oven dish and allow to cool and drain.
- In a shallow pan, gently fry the onions in 3 tbsp of oil.
- Add the remaining ingredients and stir the mixture only once before removing from the heat.
- Hold one leaf at a time in one palm of your hand whilst with the other spoon a 1 level teaspoon of the rice mixture in the center of each leaf. Fold the leaf to make a small rectangular package.
- Spread 5 vine leaves at the bottom of a shallow pan and place the dolmades side by side to in the cooking pot with the folded side facing down.
- When one layer has been completed build up layers of dolmades up to ¾ of the pot.
- Mix the rest of the olive oil with 1 cup of water and two tablespoons of lemon juice pour over the top of the “dolmades”.
- Place a layer of vine leaves across the top of the dolmades to cover them.
- Turn a side plate upside down and place it in the pot to cover most of the surface. Place the pot on a medium heat and bring to a boiling point lower the heat and simmer for 30 minutes or until there is very little water and oil in the cooking pot. (Do not cook till dry).
- Remove the plate and add the rest of the lemon juice over the dolmades.

Remove the dolmades from the pot one by one, being careful not to break them, or you can place a large deep serving plate wider than the pot over the pot and very quickly tip them over onto the serving plate, making sure the juices do not spill over. (This can be mastered). Pour more lemon juice as desired over the dolmades - Cut up quarter wedges to decorate around the plate. Serve hot with warm bread, Tzatsiki and a Greek Salad.

12. Souvlaki (Gyro)

Here we have the recipe for Greek Pita Souvlaki.
This is the most popular meal in Greece and at every Greek Festival. It is found in restaurants and found on every street corner in Greece and abroad.

INGREDIENTS

1 kg shoulder of pork (boneless) cut into bite sized cubes
10 pita breads
10 thin wooden skewers

BASTING

Juice of 1 lemon
180 ml olive oil
1 tsp salt and 1 tsp oregano mixed in a small bowl
½ tsp oregano
Salt and pepper to taste

GYRO FILLING

1 large tomato finely sliced
1 onion finely sliced and kept in a bowl with salted water
Tzatziki

PREPARATION

- Place the cubed meat in a bowl with the oil, oregano, lemon, salt, pepper, olive oil and toss over to mix well. Marinate in a bowl in the fridge for an hour or overnight.
- Thread the cubes on the skewers, placing each stick in a pan.
- Grill or barbecue over a medium heat, turning over and brushing/basting the souvlaki with a small brush with a mixture of lemon, olive oil and oregano in a small bowl. (It keeps them moist whilst cooking).
- Beat the remaining olive oil, oregano and lemon juice in a bowl.
- Place the souvlakia (plural) in a serving dish and pour the mixture over the souvlakia.
  Cover them with aluminium foil to keep them warm while you prepare the pita breads.
- Mix together 3 tablespoons of oil ½ tsp oregano and ½ tsp salt. Brush all the pita bread with the mixture and warm the pitas under the grill. Turn pita over and repeat. Do not overcook or the pita bread will harden.
- Remove the souvlaki from each skewer onto a serving dish sprinkling the juices over them.
- Place the individual plates/bowls of souvlakia, pita breads, cubed tomatoes, sliced onions, and tzatziki ready to be served.
- Each person can prepare their own souvlaki by placing the pita bread in a plate on a piece of aluminium foil and select their own filling for the pita. Roll the pita over the filling together with the aluminium. Fold down the aluminium on the pita ready to eat.
- Serve with Greek salad and fries.
- Chicken or beef can be replaced with the pork.

13. Moussaka

A very traditional Greek dish with sliced eggplant (aubergine) ground beef sauce topped with Béchamel sauce or grated cheese.

INGREDIENTS

2 medium eggplants (aubergine)
2 medium sliced potatoes
olive oil (as needed)
1 lb. lean ground beef
2 medium onions, peeled and chopped
2 tablespoons fresh minced garlic and garlic powder
1 x 8 ounce can tomato sauce
1 teaspoon dried oregano and ground nutmeg
1 teaspoon salt
1/2 teaspoon fresh ground black pepper

BÉCHAMEL SAUCE

3 tablespoons butter
1/2 teaspoon salt
1/2 teaspoon fresh ground black pepper
2 tablespoons flour
1 cup half-and-half cream
1 egg
1/2 cup grated parmesan cheese

PREPARATION

- Grease an 11 x 11-inch baking pan with olive oil. Peel the eggplants then slice 1/4-inch or so thick and season. Coat each side of sliced eggplant with olive oil and season them with salt and pepper. Place the eggplant slices on an aluminum covered cookie sheet. Broil slowly under the broiler basting with olive oil until brown; turn and broil the other side. Repeat with the sliced potato.
- In a large pot combine ground beef and onions cook stirring until it is cooked to a light brown and onions are soft. Drain the excess fat. Add in the garlic, tomato sauce, oregano, 1/2 tsp salt and black pepper to taste. When cool beat and egg and add this in to the beef (this binds it).
- On the bottom of a greased baking dish arrange potato slices to cover the bottom of the dish, sprinkle with garlic and a little nutmeg powder. Repeat the layer with half of the eggplant.
- Pour all of the ground mince mixture over the sliced eggplant layer spreading it out flat to cover this layer. (Do not use too much nutmeg because it can become bitter).
- Arrange the remaining potato slices over the ground beef mixture followed by the remaining slices of eggplant and sprinkling the layers with garlic and nutmeg powder.
- PREPARE THE BECHAMEL SAUCE:
- Melt the butter in a saucepan, whisk in flour, 1/2 tsp salt and pepper to taste. Gradually stir in half and half or milk, cook and stir over medium heat until thick and bubbly whisking continuously to avoid lumps forming.
- In a small bowl, beat the egg and stir it into the hot sauce mixing well. Add in the Parmesan cheese and stir well.
- Carefully pour the Béchamel over the Moussaka in the baking dish, making sure it does not spill over the dish. With a fork poke the Moussaka whilst the Béchamel is still hot. This helps it to even out and seep into the Moussaka.
- Baste with a beaten egg.
- Bake in a preheated oven on 180 degree C for 45 minutes or until golden brown. When the meal has cooled down, cut into squares. Do not cut when hot because it will break apart. Use a spatula to serve the portions. Serve with a Greek salad and bread.

14. Gemista

(Stuffed Tomato and Pepper)

This is a very popular dish in the summer. Although stuffed peppers and tomatoes are well known, usually we also have stuffed eggplant and zucchini.

INGREDIENTS

6 large ripe tomatoes
4 green peppers (any type of peppers are optional)
2 round eggplants
1 large zucchini
12 tablespoons well-rinsed rice (adding ground beef is optional)
2 large onions grated
1 clove garlic grated
1 bunch chopped parsley and dried oregano
1 tablespoon chopped mint
1 cup olive oil
Salt and pepper to taste

PREPARATION

- Wash the vegetables with cold water and place them in a large oven dish.
- Remove the insides of the tomatoes by slicing the very top off with a sharp knife. Scoop out the flesh, without tearing the skin.
- Do not throw away the tops that you have cut off.
- Put the flesh in a separate pan.
- Repeat the same with the peppers, zucchini and eggplant. Do not throw away the tops that you have cut off.
- Blend the tomato flesh in a food processor. Simmer tomato, onions, garlic and parsley with olive oil in a pot.
- Add the rice, seasoning and 2/3 of the olive oil, stir well and remove from the heat. (ground beef-optional)
- Season the inside of the tomatoes and vegetables. Fill the empty vegetables in the oven dish with the rice mixture from the pan, leaving a gap of ½ cm at the top of each.
- Close the tops of all the vegetables with the tops that you originally cut off.
- Dip the potatoes in the remaining 1/3 of the olive oil and add oregano, salt and pepper.
- Pour a little olive oil mixed in a little water over the stuffed vegetables.
- Bake in a pre-heated oven at 180 C for 1½ hours or until the potatoes are soft and golden.

Serve hot with fresh bread. Dipping the bread in the juices is delicious. Can be served with dolmades and Greek salad.

15. Kota Lemonati Sto Fourno Me Patates

(Lemon Chicken with Potatoes)

INGREDIENTS

Chicken

1 large chicken
1 lemon, juice of
3/4 tablespoon dried oregano
3/4 teaspoon salt
1/4 teaspoon pepper
2 garlic cloves, minced

Potatoes

5 -6 large potatoes, peeled and cut into big 1/4 wedges
1 lemon, juice of
1/2 cup olive oil
1/2 cup water
1/2 teaspoon salt
3/4 tablespoon dried oregano
1/4 teaspoon pepper
2 -3 minced garlic cloves

PREPARATION

- Wash the chicken well with lemon slices. Cut into two halves.
- Combine all the remaining ingredients and massage the chicken, inside and out, with this mixture. (There are times where I will add a little crumbled dried rosemary to the chicken and potatoes, giving the meal a tastier flavor)
- Put the chicken in a big bowl and put in the fridge while you prepare the potatoes.
- Put the potatoes and all remaining ingredients into a large baking pan. Wash your hands and put them in the pan and toss the potatoes around to coat with other ingredients.
- Place the chicken breast down in the middle of the pan surrounded by the potatoes.
- Pour the olive oil mixed in a cup of water over the chicken and potatoes.
- Bake in a pre-heated oven at 180 C for 1/2 hour or until the chicken and potatoes are golden brown.
- Keep checking regularly to make sure there is water in the pan and basting at all times.
- Remove pan and turn over the chicken – breast-side up – and continue roasting ½ hour or until chicken is nearly as golden-brown as the other side.
- Turn the oven off – don't open it, and leave the food in the oven a further 15 minutes.
- Cut chicken into serving portions and place in a serving dish surrounded by the potatoes.
- Pour the pan juices over the food decorate with lemon slices and serve hot with our Greek salad.

16. Plaki

(Baked Fish)

INGREDIENTS

7 tablespoons olive oil
olive oil, for basting and cooking
2 onions, finely chopped
2 carrots, thinly sliced
2 celery ribs, thinly sliced
2/3 cup dry white wine
1 x 14 ounce canned tomatoes with juice
pinch sugar
1 thinly sliced large lemon
2 tablespoons chopped fresh flat-leaf parsley
1 teaspoon chopped fresh marjoram
1 (2 -2 1/2 lbs) sea bass or 1 (2 -2 1/2 lbs) tilapia fillets or
1 (2 -2 1/2 lbs) red snapper, fat whole fish cleaned and scaled
(Choose your fish of preference)
salt and pepper to season

PREPARATION

- Preheat the oven to 350°.
- Oil a shallow ovenproof dish.
- Heat 4 tablespoons of oil in a pan over medium heat.
- Add the onions and garlic and cook for 5 minutes.
- Add carrots and celery.
- Cook stirring frequently for 8-10 minutes or until slightly softened.
- Remove pan from heat and pour the wine into the pan.
- Return to the stove and bring to a boil.
- Add the tomatoes with the juice, sugar, lemon slices, salt and pepper to taste. Simmer for 20 minutes then stir in the herbs.
- Put the fish in the oiled baking dish.
- Place the vegetables around the fish and arrange lemon slices on top of the fish.
- Sprinkle with the remaining oil and season to taste.
- Bake, uncovered, for 45-60 minutes depending on the thickness of the fish.

Serve immediately with Greek salad and bread.

17. Kourambiethes

(Greek Shortbread)

INGREDIENTS

650g butter
150g blanched almonds
1 kg all-purpose flour
2 egg yolks
50ml ouzo, brandy (optional) or rose water
110g icing sugar/powdered sugar
1 tsp baking powder
1g vanilla powder/essence

PREPARATION

- Place the almonds in a shallow oven dish and bake them in a pre-heated oven at 180 degrees C for about 15 minutes until slightly brown. Let them cool and then roughly chop them.
- Place the soft butter in a mixer with the icing sugar and beat thoroughly with the cake beater for 15 minutes till fluffy.
- Add the egg yolk, ouzo/rose water and vanilla powder – continue beating for another 5 minutes.
- Add the baking powder and almonds to the flour, add this mixture to the mixer and beat for a few seconds until the flour has been absorbed by the liquid.
- Take pieces of the dough; make them into the shape you prefer. Normally they are oval, but you can also make them circular, star-shaped, crescent-shaped etc. The thickness should be about 1½ cm.
- Place them on non-stick oven dishes and bake in a pre-heated oven at 160 degrees C for 20-25 minutes.
- Allow to cool, place them closely on sheet of greaseproof paper.
- Sieve plenty of icing sugar over them covering each and every one.

Traditional way – Place each one in a cake plate next to one another forming a star shape, continue placing them in a star shape with a second layer forming a pyramid shape.
These are a traditional Christmas or Easter sweet.

18. Greek Baklava

(Layers of Filo Pastry filled with Chopped Nuts and Sweetened with Syrup or Honey)

It is the best-known Greek sweet

INGREDIENTS

500g butter
300g grated walnuts or mixed nuts
40 sheets filo pastry
1 tablespoon ground cinnamon and gloves

For the syrup
650g sugar
80g glucose or lemon juice
400g water

PREPARATION

- Melt the butter in a pan.
- Butter a square oven dish start placing 20 sheets of filo pastry one at a time, brush with melted butter between each sheet as they are laid down.
- Mix the cinnamon with the walnuts - add half the mixture to the dish. Lay down 10 filo sheets.
- Add the other half of the nut mixture. Place the other 10 sheets of filo to cover the nuts again buttering in between each sheet as they are laid down.
  This makes 3 layers of filo and 2 layers of nuts.
- Place the dish in the fridge for 10 minutes.
- When you take it out, with a sharp knife cut the baklava into diamond shapes making sure it is cut right to the bottom.
- Brush the top with a butter and water mixture.
- Pre heat the oven and bake at 150 C for 90 minutes or until golden brown.

While the baklava is baking, start preparing the syrup.

- Put all the ingredients for the syrup in a pot and bring to the boil, continue boiling for 3 minutes.
- When the Baklava is removed from the oven, carefully pour the syrup evenly on the top. This has to be done when both are still hot.

Let it cool down completely before serving.
The Baklava must be covered and kept at room temperature.

19. Koulourakia

(Greek Butter Cookies with Sesame)

Koulourakia are delicious cookies dunked in coffee or tea and are also a traditionally made for Easter or Christmas.

INGREDIENTS

1 lb. soft unsalted butter
1-1/2 cups sugar
6 eggs (2 for brushing the cookies)
6 tsp. baking powder
1/2 tsp. baking soda
4 cups all-purpose flour
2 tsp. vanilla extract
2 oz. Ouzo or Fresh orange juice
Sesame seeds (optional)

PREPARATION

- Preheat the oven to 350 degrees.
- Using the mixer, beat the butter and sugar until light and fluffy. Add the vanilla extract and ouzo/orange juice and mix well. While the mixer is running, add eggs one by one and mix until fluffy and have combined well.
- In a separate bowl, sift the flour with the baking powder and soda.
- Add the flour mixture to the butter mixture a little at a time. The dough will be soft and pliable, it should not be sticky. You should be able to pinch off a ball of dough and roll it into a small ball, cord or thin tube without breaking.
- If the dough is still sticky, add a little more flour. Allow the dough to rest a bit before rolling into shapes.
- To shape the cookies, pinch off a piece of dough about the size of a walnut. Roll into a ball make oval shapes, “S” shape or roll out a cord or thin tube of dough into a 6” length; fold this in half and twist. You can also make a coiled circle.
- (Shape to your preference)
- Place onto a lightly greased baking sheet about 1” apart.
- Beat the remaining two eggs in a bowl with a splash of water. Lightly brush the cookies with the egg wash and sprinkle with sesame seeds (optional).
- Bake at 350 F degrees for approximately 20 minutes or until slightly golden brown.
- Arrange on a platter or store in a baking tin.

20. Loukoumathes

(Small Honey Balls)

INGREDIENTS

2 large eggs
3/4 cup milk
2 cups all-purpose flour
1 teaspoon baking powder
Honey and water with 1 teaspoon of lemon juice (for drizzling)
Ground cinnamon
Finely chopped walnuts or roasted sesame seed

PREPARATION

- Beat the eggs well and add milk add sifted flour and baking powder. Stir with a wooden spoon until the mixture is smooth and not lumpy.

- Heat 2-3 inches of vegetable oil in a deep saucepan or deep frying pan to a medium to high heat.

- When the oil is hot, gently drop a teaspoonful of batter into the oil and gently fry turning the doughnut with a fork until light golden on all sides.

- **Tip:** Keep a small bowl of cold water next to the workspace and dip finger before pushing batter into the oil (to keep batter from sticking).

- Place them on a paper towel to drain.

- Boil the honey and water ½ and ½, drop with the lemon juice, drop in the doughnuts, roll and let them soak for a minute. If desired drizzle with honey and sprinkle with nuts, ground cinnamon and roasted sesame seed.

- Serve when hot.

21. Ravani

(Sweet Semolina Cake)

This is a traditional Greek cake serve with Greek coffee or tea.

INGREDIENTS

6 eggs (separate the whites and yolks)
2 ¼ cups sugar
2 ¼ cups flour
2 ¼ cups semolina
1/2 teaspoon baking powder
1/4 cup grated lemon rind

Syrup

9 cups sugar
7 cups water
2 vanilla beans (do not cut open) or vanilla essence
Juice of 1/2 lemon

PREPARATION

Cake

- Whisk the egg whites into a fluffy meringue and add the egg yolk.
- Add the sugar, flour, baking powder, and semolina and lemon rind. Mix well.
- Pour into a large greased baking pan.

Bake for about 45 minutes at 180 C.
Leave to cool and prepare the syrup.

Syrup

- Bring the water and sugar to a boil with the vanilla and lemon juice.
- Gently boil for 5 minutes.
- Leave the cake in the baking pan cut into square pieces and pour the syrup over it.
- Let the syrup soak in and let the "Ravani" cool to room temperature before serving.
- Decorate with coconut or powdered sugar. (optional)
- The cake can be kept covered in the fridge.

ABOUT THE AUTHOR

I, Anna Othitis, am Greek by birth, born on the Island of Rhodes, Greece to Greek parents. My mother is from the Island of Crete and my father from the Island of Kasos. I grew up in my town of Gweru in the beautiful country of Zimbabwe, Africa. I married George, whose parents were from the Island of Karpathos. So I call myself an African originating from the Dodecanese Islands of Greece. My three children, Johnny, Elia and Frankie, were born and grew up in Gweru. Now we are recent residents of New Jersey, USA.

All of my life, since being a young girl, I have loved cooking and baking our traditional and authentic Greek meals and have loved entertaining friends and family with Greek food.

I clearly remember as a five-year-old sitting by my grandmother's side helping her roll her special "dolmathes" (the cabbage rolled leaves) and baking and cooking with her.

My mother always believed that we had to learn to be domesticated to cook and bake so that one day we could take care of our husbands and own families. The typical Greek old traditional way of a girl's upbringing.

As a married lady I loved learning the various dishes and learned all the traditional cooking and baking of the island of Karpathos from my mother-in-law, Franga.

Cooking comes naturally to me and I enjoy experimenting with new ingredients and recipes in my Greek cooking.

Home Cooked and Baked

By

Anna Othitis

Printed in Great Britain
by Amazon.co.uk, Ltd.,
Marston Gate.